T0209558

THE MARRIAGE GUIDE

God Ordains It, You Establish It

♥ ♥ ♥ ♥ ♥ ♥

Walter Carter Sr. and Valecia Carter

WESTBOW
PRESS®
A DIVISION OF THOMAS NELSON
& ZONDERVAN

WestBow Press books may be ordered through booksellers or by contacting:

WestBow Press
A Division of Thomas Nelson & Zondervan
1663 Liberty Drive
Bloomington, IN 47403
www.westbowpress.com
844-714-3454

Interior Image Credit: Roche' Buford/Project One Studios

Scripture taken from the King James Version of the Bible.

Scripture quotations marked (NLT) are taken from the Holy Bible, New Living Translation, copyright ©1996, 2004, 2015 by Tyndale House Foundation. Used by permission of Tyndale House Publishers, a Division of Tyndale House Ministries, Carol Stream, Illinois 60188. All rights reserved.

Scripture quotations taken from The Holy Bible, New International Version® NIV® Copyright © 1973 1978 1984 2011 by Biblica, Inc. TM. Used by permission. All rights reserved worldwide.

Scripture quotations are from the ESV® Bible (The Holy Bible, English Standard Version®), copyright © 2001 by Crossway, a publishing ministry of Good News Publishers. Used by permission. All rights reserved.

Scripture taken from the Amplified Bible, Copyright © 1954, 1958, 1962, 1964, 1965, 1987 by The Lockman Foundation. Used with permission.

Scripture quotations taken from the (NASB®) New American Standard Bible®, Copyright © 1960, 1971, 1977, 1995, 2020 by The Lockman Foundation. Used by permission. All rights reserved. www.lockman.org

ISBN: 978-1-6642-6223-2 (sc)
ISBN: 978-1-6642-6222-5 (e)

Library of Congress Control Number: 2022905868

Print information available on the last page.

WestBow Press rev. date: 05/23/2022

CONTENTS

Thank You vii
Foreword ix
Preface xi
Introduction xv

Chapter 1 1
Questions to Ask Before and After "I Do"

Chapter 2 3
Reflect and Reminisce

Chapter 3 15
Vision and Mission

Chapter 4 23
The Honeymoon Phase

Chapter 5 27
Building Your Foundation

Chapter 6 33
Budget or Bust

Chapter 7 43
The In-and-Out Phase

Chapter 8 49
Unexpected Circumstances

Chapter 9 55
Intimate Moments

Chapter 10 63
The Marriage Plan

Acknowledgments 65
Scriptures Cited 67
About the Authors 69

Thank You

♥ ♥ ♥ ♥ ♥ ♥

We are elated to have been able to write this amazing teaching tool and guide. Without the Lord we would not have been able to complete the task of writing this informative marriage guide together. God has elevated us and set our standards higher than we ever could have imagined. The path God set before us is not one we take lightly, and we do not take it for granted. We will always seek him because we know he has us in his care, especially since he saved and blessed our marriage! We thank you, we appreciate you, and we love you!

Foreword

♥ ♥ ♥ ♥ ♥ ♥

Scripture states, "Therefore shall a man leave his father and his mother and shall cleave unto his wife: and they shall be one flesh" (Genesis 2:24 KJV).

"One flesh," the remarkable result in which the plural becomes singular—a separate heart now bonds with another and embarks on an incredible journey through the covenant of marriage. Authors Valecia and Walter Carter bring those words to life. Being married for well over twenty-four years is an inspiration, and the fabulous pair is still going strong. When you see them together, their love is always on display; there is this in-depth understanding of each other, an authentic example of oneness. In addition to the training they received as certified marriage coaches, weaved deep within the fabric of their strong relationship is priceless information gained by both God's Word and hands-on experience. I believe it is God's will for them to share lessons learned; therefore, I am delighted they have written *The Marriage Guide: God Ordains It, You Establish It*.

I understand that each reader approaches this book from different places. For some, it may be how to strengthen the bond between you and your mate; or maybe healing is needed, and you are looking for the best way to start an honest conversation and forgive. Others may have found the person they want to spend the rest of their lives with, and they seek godly counsel to equip themselves and their future spouse with biblical principles for sustained bliss. Regardless of where you are, *The Marriage Guide: God Ordains It, You Establish It* will provide the tools necessary to keep the flame of love burning until death do you part.

What separates this book from others is the gift God has bestowed upon the Carters to share this knowledge with the world in a down-to-earth style while maintaining the richness and integrity deserving of a divinely ordained union. Words like "transparency" and "genuineness" may come to mind as they address problematic situations of the past that posed threats to end their marriage and what it took to overcome them. I appreciate how they display care about the reader's success; revealing their stories provides crisis prevention strategies by exploring the heart's deep matters.

I have the privilege of knowing authors Valecia and Walter Carter personally; the motivation behind their conviction is helping others. That belief led to them establishing Above the Heart LLC, which has blessed many; there is no doubt *The Marriage Guide: God Ordains It, You Establish It* will do the same.

Pastor Jeremy L. Gilbert

Preface

♥ ♥ ♥ ♥ ♥ ♥

Ecclesiastes 4:9–12 (NLT) says:

> Two people are better off than one, for they can help each other succeed. If one person falls, the other can reach out and help. But someone who falls alone is in real trouble. Likewise, two people lying close together can keep each other warm. But how can one be warm alone? A person standing alone can be attacked and defeated, but two can stand back-to-back and conquer. Three are even better, for a triple-braided cord is not easily broken.

This scripture will help you lean on each other and work on reaching your goals together with success. When we launched our marriage-coaching business, my husband addressed our attendees by explaining the purpose of Above the Heart LLC. He illustrated by having us stand arm in arm, facing opposite ways and trying to walk in different directions. Of course, that did not work, but once we stood with linked arms in the same direction and walked side by side, we were able to get somewhere. He also had us stand back to back, and then we were able to see everything from all sides. He covered my back, and I covered his. Words alone may not express the message displayed at the time, but everyone in attendance was touched by his words of wisdom, and I thank God every day for blessing him with such insight and truth.

When you meet your soulmate, what determines that this person is "the one"? Why is it that sometimes a person gets married several times before realizing who their actual soulmate is? There can be several reasons the vows you make on your wedding day are not honored until death actually does part you. We are not judging anyone, because at times circumstances may result in your parting by way of divorce. We do believe that if you give yourselves time to know each other and learn what the other one is really like, you will have a clearer view of whether you are soulmates or not. Do not be quick to jump into a marriage without considering all factors. Do not get married just to prevent sinning because you feel you cannot resist the temptation of having premarital sex. Marriage is so much more than that. God ordained marriage, and the vows state that it is a lifelong covenant. If you keep God at the forefront through the ups and downs, it will be a success. God does not make mistakes; *we* mess up when we try to tell God our plan instead of following his plan.

One perfect example is a devastating time when we struggled within our marriage and I had my husband served with a restraining order. Some of our children were still very young, and we were actively going to church on a regular basis while living in separate houses. I informed the pastor of the situation and told him that my husband could not attend the church anymore because with the restraining order in place, he could not be within one hundred feet of me.

I handed our pastor the court document, and after he read it, he put it in his desk and said, "I understand what this restraining order says, but I will not tell your husband he cannot attend his own church. I don't care what this court document says, because I have an obligation to God to save souls, and this man has a soul that needs saving. So what I can do is have one of you sit in the balcony, and the other one sit downstairs. I will make sure you are kept apart, but I will never keep him from coming to church. That will not help him get closer to God or help him with the issues he has, and as your pastor I have to follow God and do things his way."

I was so upset when he said that, but I did understand what he said and why he said it. After I thought about it, I was more compassionate about him coming to church, and it did make a lot of sense after I got out of my feelings. We went through this for months, with him sitting in the balcony and me sitting downstairs in the second row. It was such an uncomfortable, painful situation, but because we separately focused on God for ourselves and lived according to God's will, we were able to overcome this heavy time in our marriage. We have so many circumstances we have faced together, and it took God to help us through them all. That's why we want to help others help themselves so they too can have the best marriage or relationship they desire.

Valecia Carter

Introduction

♥ ♥ ♥ ♥ ♥ ♥

In our technique of marriage coaching, we focus on the discipline of believing in a couple and engaging with them to see where God is motivating them to grow or change while keeping them responsible for the process. This book was created through our experience and training by God's direction. This guide is a learning tool based on biblical principles of marriage. It offers suggestions and scenarios to give you some insight on how we handled circumstances we faced. Working through this book will help you take your marriage or relationship to the next level. This book is for those who are married or engaged and for singles who aspire to be married.

There is a difference between marriage/relationship coaching and marriage/relationship counseling. Counselors spend a fair amount of time focusing on understanding and examining past problems to help couples make changes or do things differently. Don't get me wrong: there are times when circumstances make it necessary to revisit situations and come to a resolution concerning the past in order to move forward. Coaches help couples assess various areas of their marriage or relationship in the present to help it progress in the future, to perfect your plan for success in your endeavors and goals. We focus on getting into the grit of coaching with our clients because of the importance of their receiving the necessary strategies, advice, and tools to help get to where they need to be in their marriage or relationship. Your success is our goal. Since you are reading the marriage guide, you seem to be ready to get your relationship where you want it to be, and this tool will help you get things in order.

Our coaching method is more action-oriented and consistent in helping you move forward, as we have our clients do self-reflection projects, assignments, and relationship-building exercises, to name a few techniques. Hands-on processes helped us in our marriage success, and we believe it will help enhance your marriage or relationship as well. You cannot move ahead if you are constantly looking back—our process is much shorter and more task-based. And when the focus is on what you want your relationship to be, the coaching sessions are much more positive and future-oriented. As your coaches, we will actively participate in helping you acquire what you need to stay focused on your goal of having the best marriage or relationship you desire!

Have you ever considered life without a plan? What would your life look like if you failed to plan any and everything? Take a minute to reflect on how different your life would be if you either started or stopped planning for any of the following: outfits for the week, your daily routine, chores, exercise, outings, vacations, parties, weddings, funerals, retirement … do you have a plan for these, or have you ever planned for any of them? Did things run more smoothly when you had a plan? If you said yes, I would agree with you, because whenever we plan out whatever it is, things come together much better. The definition of *plan* in my dictionary is "a detailed proposal for doing or achieving something." It is important to plan anything you want to be successful.

We write out plans in our lives with the smallest details, and if you want to start a business, you don't just start it on a whim. A wise entrepreneur will write a business plan and follow it for success. A marriage plan is an outline and guide to what a successful marriage looks like. That is why we suggest you write out your marriage plan *and follow it*.

Marriage is a lifetime commitment ordained by God. It just makes sense to write out your marriage plan when you are looking to take that step. Ephesians 5:22-26 (NIV) says:

> Wives, submit yourselves to your own husbands as you do to the Lord. For the husband is the head of the wife as Christ is the head of the church, his body, of which he is the Savior. Now as the church submits to Christ, so also wives should submit to their husbands in everything. Husbands, love your wives, just as Christ loved the church and gave himself up for her to make her holy, cleansing her by the washing with water through the word.

God gives us direct instructions for our roles as husband and wife, so there isn't any question as long as we follow God's plan first!

Before you become a couple, you are an individual, so at times you will express your own individuality. Don't think that you always have to submerge your own voice. Your personality and uniqueness play a great role in your union together, and as you read on, you will gain more perspective both as an individual and as the manifestation of a couple. In each chapter we give you at least one hands-on exercise, scenario, or example, which is an essential feature of our coaching method. It doesn't matter if you are in a coaching session with us one on one, or if you are thousands of miles away, these self-reflection projects, assignments, and relationship-building exercises are essential in our coaching strategies, and we know you will benefit from these techniques when you apply them to your life.

We decided to write this book in the hope of helping others reach their goals in their marriage or relationship. We went through many unsavory circumstances through the course of our marriage, and things may have been a lot less complicated if we had discussed our short- and long-term goals and written out our marriage plan. Not long ago, we sat and talked about how God saved and blessed our marriage after the trials and tribulations we faced during our first fifteen years. God put it on our hearts to write a book with a guide to help put things in perspective and keep you on the right track by getting together, focusing on each other, and writing down what will work best for the two of you. Once we put God first and sought him daily, things were clearer and made more sense. *The Marriage Guide* has helped us, and we don't doubt that it will help you, so thank you for taking time to invest in yourself and your marriage or relationship!

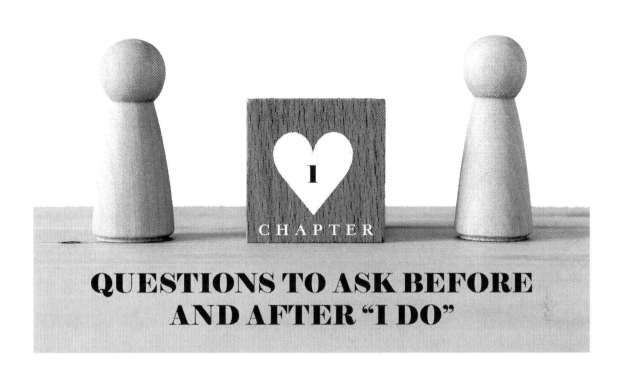

QUESTIONS TO ASK BEFORE AND AFTER "I DO"

Before you commit to a relationship with each other, the two of you should be honest about who you are and about your relationship with the Lord. Were you and your mate in the world together? What do you do if after being married your spouse gives their life to the Lord? What are you going to do if you are saved, but your mate is not?

A lot of people feel that when you give your life to the Lord, your mate should automatically do the same thing, but it does not work that way just because you may want it to. Just as it took you time to give your life to God, now you need to activate your faith, trust in the Lord, and be patient. Things do not happen in our time; everything will happen in God's time, and your mate must want to do it willingly. You should not pressure your mate or give them an ultimatum. These tactics will make the situation worse—it will not draw them in but may push them away.

We trust God to wake us up every morning, and we trust God with our job security and our everyday carrying on, so why is it so challenging for us to trust God with the circumstances that we face in our marriage? Most of us are too quick to give up instead of waiting for God to move on our behalf. Everything will work out just as God intends if we do as I Peter 3:1-2 (AMP) says:

In the same way, you wives, be submissive to your own husbands [subordinate, not as inferior, but out of respect for the responsibilities entrusted to husbands and their accountability to God, and so partnering with them] so that even if some do not obey the word [of God], they may be won over [to Christ] without discussion by the godly lives of their wives, when they see your modest and respectful behavior [together with your devotion and appreciation—love your husband, encourage him, and enjoy him as a blessing from God].

It isn't our job to put a time frame on someone giving their life to the Lord. God was patient with you, so extend that same level of patience by continuing to pray for your spouse. Stand in the gap, and don't fuss or complain. Continue to be loving and kind and let your light shine. Remember, if you do your part and handle God's business every day by giving him some of your time by praying, reading the Bible, and seeking him, he will handle your business concerning your home and family. We start our day with God together in prayer, and we pray together before going to bed.

Whether you are already married or planning to get married, following are some questions to ask yourselves.

1. How do you handle stress?
2. Does my spouse or mate have any hang-ups (such as drugs, cigarettes, alcohol, lying, or gambling)?
3. How do you handle conflict?
4. How do you handle your finances?
5. How will you divide household chores?
6. What if you both want different things, and you can't afford both? How will you choose?
7. How will you make decisions? Will you discuss and make decisions together?
8. If you have separate church homes, will you serve together and receive the same teaching, or will you continue to worship separately?
9. If you will be a blended family, how will you make sure all the children feel they are part of the family? Or if no children are involved, will there be in-laws, and what role will your mate's extended family play in your new life together? Will your relationship to faith be an influence?
10. How do you feel about your mate being friends with the opposite sex, and when does that become emotional infidelity to you?

REFLECT AND REMINISCE

It's important in a relationship to have that dialogue between the two of you, so at times we will be conducting a conversation that will allow you to see us speaking one at a time.

WALTER: One important component to consider while reflecting and reminiscing is the first moment you noticed each other. Think about how you met, what you were doing when you met, and what it was that you liked about each other. Was it an instant attraction, or did you grow to like each other? What do you admire about your mate? Take this time to list what you like about each other. It is a good thing to brag on your mate right here. Go all the way back to the beginning, and be generous.

What I want you as the reader to know is that when I, Walter Carter Sr., met my future wife, I liked so many things about her. I liked that Valecia was *fine*; I liked her smile, her eyes, and lips. I learned that she loves family and loves to cook. I like her positive attitude, her compassion for others, and her thoughtfulness. I like that she loves to have fun. When we met, I admired that she was a responsible single mother who worked, took care of her home, had a nice car, and depended on herself.

The purpose of this exercise is to have a list of the positives, so that when you have situations that test your love, you can reflect and reminisce about the good times that outweigh those not-so-good times you may be facing currently or in the future.

VALECIA: Now that you heard from my husband, let me list some things about him. I liked that Walter was goal-oriented and driven. He knew what he wanted and went after it. He cared for his children, and he's old fashioned in a good way—he worked and paid his bills and lived in his own place. He was so handsome too! I admired that he put others before himself and believed in taking care of his wife and family.

I had always thought that a great wedding was when a man and a woman said their vows to each other in the presence of God with their family and friends witnessing them unite as one, and then they were wished well as they go on and live happily ever after. At least that is what I thought it was! Walter and I fell in love and decided to get married regardless of those who were against us. When we announced that we were getting married, we weren't expecting the reaction we received from our so-called friends, but I guess they had reasons to be concerned. In their eyes, we were not supposed to make it together. They had voted us out and literally bet against us—we found out that several of Walter's friends didn't show up to our wedding because they had a bet to see how soon our marriage would end. This weighed heavily on us because we always felt that a true friend will accept and respect your decisions and support you whether they agree with your choices or not. We kind of felt abandoned and alone when those we thought were really close weren't there to celebrate our union. There were several negative thoughts about us from our friends when we got married. How they handled our decision to get married seemed rather harsh, but they stood by what they felt and didn't show up to our wedding. There were many unpleasant circumstances that we faced during the first fifteen years of our marriage, and the average couple most likely would have given up a long time ago.

When I used to hang out with Walter at his bachelor pad with his friends, aka "the clique," we would all sit around, listen to music, and drink. One thing about the clique was that you could count on a lot of drinking going on when you went around. We were all young and having fun, so we thought nothing of it. It wasn't until we started to get older and the drinking continued that a problem arose.

Walter didn't see himself as an abuser or a man with a drinking problem. He thought that he had everything under control. At times when I expressed my concern about his drinking, he would slow down a little, but that wouldn't last long. He would start right back drinking like a fish soon after, and then more issues would arise.

One day my sisters were at our house with me, and we were sitting around laughing and talking when Walter came home. It was clear to us he was intoxicated from drinking. I was so irritated. I asked him why he was drinking, and he said he hadn't been, so that started the argument. He tried to walk away, but I grabbed his arm and took his keys from him so he wouldn't be able to come back to the house. I wanted him to leave. He snatched the keys from me, and I almost fell down. I hit him with the sweeper, and he grabbed me. Then my sisters grabbed him and yelled, "Don't touch our sister!" In a drunken slur, he yelled, "She hitting me!" I told him he should leave because I was sick of him constantly coming in and out drunk. He went to go pack some clothes, and he hurried up and got out of there.

I laugh at this now because I can remember seeing him walking quickly down the alley carrying my yellow suitcase with purple and blue flowers all over it.

We have gone through counseling several times during our marriage. I want to tell you about a particular time with a pastor who was a marriage counselor and therapist for a living. He got paid to counsel people, so to give you an understanding, whenever we went to him we paid him. There was a time when Walter and I were supposed to go to our counseling session, and when I went to pick him up, I saw him sitting on the porch at his friend's house. When he saw me pulling up he ran into his friend's house. I asked his friend to tell Walter to please come out so we could go. He said Walter wasn't there. I told him I saw him run into the house. Walter did not come back outside, so I went to the session alone. The pastor told me that since Walter and I couldn't get it together enough to come to the sessions, he was no longer interested in counseling us, and he suggested that we get a divorce.

I was shocked. I could not believe that this was a man of the cloth who was basically telling me to give up on my marriage. I felt alone and lifeless, and for a while I just let things be the way they were. I started to fall on my knees and ask God to take control of my life because I did not have a handle on it. That was the last time we went to him for counseling.

The scenarios I'm recalling were after we were already married, but believe me when I tell you that we had many unhealthy arguments and situations before we were married. As I reflect and reminisce, although there were a lot of not-so-good times, there were a lot of particularly good times, which is why I continued to hold on.

Now it is your turn to reflect on your past. Think about when you first met or when the attraction began. This is the time to really dig deep and enjoy reminiscing. Let Walter and me expound a little by telling you about how we first met. I hope this will give you insight into how we reflect and reminisce.

Walter and I met at my job. It was not a sudden attraction, but he was interesting. I liked that he had a leadership role in his job—did I mention he was handsome?—and he was very direct when he had something to say. Well, that part I was not a fan of, but there were more things that I liked about him than things I disliked about him.

WALTER: As I was working with my stilts on mudding and taping the ceiling in the conference room, I couldn't help but notice Valecia. As she walked through the room to go make copies, I was attracted to her beauty. It was at that moment I knew I had to get to know her.

VALECIA: As time went on, we saw each other at work daily. The more we saw each other, the more we conversed, and before I knew it, we were dating. It was a lot to consider because I had never dated anyone from work before. But I guessed it was OK, since he was an outside contractor who was only working there until the conference room was complete.

WALTER: I noticed a difference in Valecia from the other women I dated. Some were just fun to hang out with, but it was different with Valecia. We had only been dating for one week when I knew she was marriage material. A woman has certain qualities that appeal to a man when he knows what he's looking for in a wife, and I knew she was the one.

VALECIA: I admire so many things about my husband. To name a few, he took care of me and our children the best way he could, even while he was struggling with his addiction. I admire his love for his children, his ambition and determination to reach his goals, his love for Christ, his intellect, and how he takes his time to think about things before making any major decisions.

WALTER: What I admire about my wife is the love and kindness she shares, her motherly qualities, her determination, her drive to do the things she sets her mind to, and her ability to keep going and not give up when things get tough. She may drive me crazy sometimes with her emotional ways and the tears she cries whether she's happy, sad, upset, or just watching a movie, but we balance each other well, and I love her deeply.

Proverbs 18:22 (AMP) says, "He who finds a [true and faithful] wife finds a good thing and obtains favor and approval from the Lord." This scripture is to let you know that God is pleased with your marriage, so value it and keep the good times flowing. Don't forget how great things were when you decided to get married.

Now it is time to do some reflecting and reminiscing of your own. These next two exercises will allow you to dig deep as you go back to the time when you first met and were in the beginning stages of your relationship. Your lists do not have to be identical—in fact, the point is that you each list your own memories and thoughts. These are *your* moments, and sharing them will bring up a lot of exciting conversation between the two of you.

What I like about him	What I like about her
1.	1.
2.	2.
3.	3.
4.	4.
5.	5.

6.	6.
7.	7.
8.	8.
9.	9.
10.	10.
11.	11.
12.	12.

What I admire about him	What I admire about her
1.	1.
2.	2.
3.	3.
4.	4.
5.	5.
6.	6.

7.	7.
8.	8.
9.	9.
10.	10.

Remembering what brought you together and led to your decision to become husband and wife is relevant and necessary to maintaining your relationship. What you did to *get* each other is what you need to do to *keep* each other. List what your spouse did that you loved, and put a star next to what they still do.

I love that he ...	I love that she ...

Valecia Carter
Certified Marriage
Breakthrough Coach,
Author,
& Motivational Speaker

Walter Carter, Sr.
Certified Marriage
Breakthrough Coach
& Motivational Speaker

Christian Living

Christian Indie Awards

2019 Winner
Nonfiction Christian
Living Category

Walter & Valecia Carter

VISION AND MISSION

When we got married, we didn't have any idea what marriage was really all about. We wanted to live together, and all the talking we were doing about this and that screamed longevity. We thought that if you loved someone enough to be together as long as we had been, you were destined for a great marriage. We didn't think about credit scores, purchasing a home, our careers, expanding our family, possibly relocating to another state, or anything of importance. We based our decision to marry on the pure fact that we loved each other, and we'd figure out the rest on our journey.

We don't recommend that you do it the way we did! See, we were young when we got married, and we thought we had it all figured out. Boy, were we mistaken.

VALECIA: We didn't know a lot about many things pertaining to maintaining a successful marriage, and I blame that on our lack of preparation. I imagined a fairy tale wedding from childhood with a happily-ever-after lifestyle that carried onto adulthood. Then I experienced the sudden heartbreak and disappointment of it on our wedding day, as I hope you will understand as you read more.

It was August 3, 1996—a bright and sunny hot day! I woke up excited that I was going to be married in a matter of hours. If you read my book *My Heart, My Love, My Life, My*

Lord: Living Life Past the Pain, you already know how things went from my perspective, so here's how the day went from Walter's view.

WALTER: I woke up feeling pumped up because the woman I met four years ago and fell in love with was about to become my wife. I felt like the luckiest man alive. My day was moving pretty smooth to start. All I had to do was get up, shower, decorate the van, get dressed, and head to the church. I thought I was all set until my soon-to-be wife called me to ask about the undecorated hall where we were having the wedding reception. I honestly forgot all about me and my guys decorating the hall, but this would just be the first of many more hiccups. I arrived at the church, wondering why all our family and friends were standing around outside talking in the heat. I asked if they were coming in, and they told me the church doors were locked. I went to open the door, and yes, they were locked. I banged and banged and banged on the door, but nobody opened it.

I waited outside the church until finally the doors opened, and apparently there was another couple getting married, using our decorations. I was trying to get answers, and nobody would comply. Time went on, and it was after 3:30 p.m. and still no bride. So now I am getting worried. I know she's not going to stand me up, but where is she?

It's now 3:45 p.m., and I was told my bride was there getting her makeup done. A few minutes later I get word that she has left some key items at the house, so I jumped in the van and drove to the house as fast as I could. I grabbed everything, jumped back on the freeway, got to the church, and noticed that every decoration we put on our van was no longer there— just the colorful stubs were still stuck on under the tape. I guess the freeway blew them away.

I got the items to my beautiful bride, and then I was told by the singer that he had to leave. He said he had a strip gig in another nearby city. I was shocked, because I knew nothing about him being a singer and a stripper.

Arrangements were made for my bride's cousin to sing, and now the wedding starts. I see the flower girl come down the aisle before the ushers pull down the aisle runner, so the flowers were all underneath on the floor. But when I saw my wife to be walking down the aisle to me, not one of the disasters mattered. She was stunning, and seeing her smile brought tears to my eyes. I was so excited to be marrying the love of my life.

When her cousin got up to sing, I know Valecia wanted "The Lord's Prayer," but the song she sang was "Precious Lord," which I know is usually a choice for funerals, but we were just grateful she sang on the spot. We said our vows, were pronounced man and wife, and were on our way to the reception hall, blowing the horn and drawing attention because we just got married … when our horn burned out. We looked at each other in disbelief. How in the world could so many horrible things go wrong on our wedding day?

We wanted to tell you about our wedding day because none of it turned out the way we expected it to—it was not planned with attention to detail. It was more or less thrown together in a few months. From the officiant who couldn't marry us because she fell ill the day before our wedding, down to the horn from the car going out on us and not working, before, during, and after the wedding, everything seemed to go wrong. It doesn't matter so much as we think about it now, and all we should have cared about at the time was celebrating our union with family and friends at the reception, but it definitely was the start to many challenges we would face. Planning your wedding is a way you can express what your vision for your marriage should be, since planning requires communication, cooperation, time and patience. Make sure you are focused and ready to put in the work.

What does a healthy marriage look, sound, and act like to you? For us, a healthy marriage is spending quality time together; for instance, we eat meals together as a family without outside interruptions. No electronic devices, no television, and no cell phones are allowed at the table. We have family meetings twice a month, as we did when the children were still living at home, and we have weekly date nights, which doesn't always require spending money. We have picnics on a blanket in our bedroom complete with our picnic basket, or we watch a movie cuddling in front of the fireplace, eating homemade popcorn and drinking sparkling grape juice. We are so in tune with each other's needs, and we laugh, joke, play, and have a powerful prayer life.

We pray together multiple times every day, and we worship God together. It is vital for us to have fellowship together, hearing God's word as a unit, because we are living proof of the power of God manifesting and growing in both our lives—we have been with one accord in Christ. We respect each other by listening and getting an understanding with an open heart and mind. All couples disagree, and we all argue, but arguing shouldn't be malicious or cruel. There are healthy ways to argue. Use fair fighting words, and refrain from using harsh, painful words. Speak to your mate the way you want to be spoken to. Arguing is a great outlet because it is a form of communication, but focus on your strengths, be kind to each other, and continue to be attracted to your spouse.

Strength in marriage draws on many attributes, including healthy communication, good problem-solving skills, and setting boundaries for each other to honor. For example, when we argue and it is getting heated, we stop, take a break, and revisit the disagreement later, but we don't leave the house—we just take a break, go to different rooms, and give ourselves time to calm down and look at the circumstances from the other person's perspective.

At times when we have an argument, we look back and laugh at how simple or small what we were arguing about was. But we have also realized it's the little arguments that help us resolve bigger arguments with respect and compassion—and that leads to romance and intimacy, also known as make-up sex.

You must know what your mate likes! It could be a certain hairstyle or color, that certain cologne or perfume, a style of clothing, or a favorite dessert or meal you make. It's to your advantage to surprise your mate with their favorite something "just because." It's like lighting a scented candle: as the candle burns and the flame moves down into the scented wax, the sweet aroma drifts through and fills the air, giving you that satisfying conclusion you were patiently waiting for. Imagine coming home one day and your spouse has a favorite something to surprise you with. How would that make you feel? Sounds like the beginning of a perfect evening!

Colossians 3:12–14 (NASB) says:

> So, as those who have been chosen of God, holy and beloved, put on a heart of compassion, kindness, humility, gentleness, and patience; bearing with one another, and forgiving each other, whoever has a complaint against anyone; just as the Lord forgave you, so must you do also. In addition to all these things put on love, which is the perfect bond of unity.

You may want to connect with a successful married couple, so you can gain knowledge and useful tools that might be applied in your own marriage. We aren't saying you should model your marriage after another couple's—just advising you to connect and continue to offer suggestions to one another. If you see something positive or helpful that is working for a successful married couple you associate with, what can you learn from their marriage?

Now that you have discussed some of your goals, take some time to write them down and consolidate your vision. Before you can prepare your vision, you have to communicate with each other, so that this vision is a combination of what you both want. You can start by discussing what you are aiming for and compiling a list of goals. We recommend that you create a vision board. If you are not familiar with a vision board, it's a tool to help clarify and maintain focus on what truly matters to you—a physical board on which you display images that represent what you want to be, do, or have in your life. You can use poster board, markers, pen or pencil, and something for a decorative border. You can make a border out of any material, stencils, or clippings from magazines. You can get as creative as you like, as long as you do it together. Make it fun and appealing. This board will be posted somewhere in your home where you will see it every day to remind you of what you are aiming for. It will be a great inspiration and motivator to help you achieve your goals. You may have another method in mind, and that will be just fine. The goal is to have something in physical that you can put up on a wall, visible daily as a reminder to push you to reach your goal.

One important component is to find scripture to be governed by. This is for your entire household! A great scripture that we found to be amazing for our family is Joshua 24:15 (KJV):

> And if it seem evil unto you to serve the Lord, choose you this day whom ye will serve; whether the gods which your fathers served that were on the other side of the flood, or the gods of the Amorites, in whose land ye dwell: but as for me and my house, we will serve the Lord.

Here is one template for your vision board, but remember—be as creative in how you put together your board as you want your relationship to be.

Vision Board

Short-term goals	Long-term goals	Scripture/ inspiration	Miscellaneous notes

THE HONEYMOON PHASE

The honeymoon phase is when everything seems perfect. During this time, you are so in love and in tune with each other that nothing else seems to matter. You are more accepting of each other's flaws and may even deem them, at most times, to be cute. You feel as if you are living out your very own fairy tale and that it's all happily ever after.

The honeymoon phase usually lasts from eighteen to twenty-four months. During this time, your communication is vibrant and filled with affection. It's one of the most interesting times of a relationship. Everything seems exhilarating, brand new, and extremely promising. It's like when you were dating, and you stayed up for hours just talking on the phone, debating who would hang up first. Well, that is how you feel during the honeymoon phase. The love is hot like a flame, filled with passion and ecstasy. Date nights are more excessive in the beginning, and you don't care where you go or what you do, just as long as you are together. You take your lunch breaks together if you can, or you call each other on your breaks. You don't mind going on shopping trips together and are even willing to go to barber or beauty shop appointments. During the honeymoon phase, you can't get enough of each other, whether it's a phone call or intimacy. You are both so understanding about almost everything. There are no issues you can't surpass in your eyes as you pine over each other daily.

If you are in the honeymoon phase of your relationship, it's the perfect time to create memories by taking lots of pictures and videos and by documenting the events, outings, and special occasions that you share. When times get tough during the course of your marriage, you can revisit your memories and push past the present issue with recollections of wonderful times. The honeymoon phase could very well be short-lived if you aren't mindful.

When you do start to have more disagreements in your marriage, address every circumstance head on. Don't just sweep it under the rug. Covering it up will not resolve it. If you avoid addressing the issues, your marriage will be in trouble. Remember, as we discussed in chapter 3, it is OK to argue *in the right way*. That is a sign of a healthy marriage. Keeping things bottled up inside is a quick path to an unnecessary major explosion.

One reason everything seems so exciting and new when you are getting to know so much about each other is that it is all still a mystery. The thrill of discovering everything that you can about each other makes you want to spend more and more time together. You want to be intimate physically and to learn about each other's past, present, and future. You are intrigued with the other person's uniqueness and quaint personality. You get those butterflies in your stomach at a mere thought of them, your hormones are at a heightened level, and your connection is stronger than you can imagine. Everything is mysterious … until you learn all there is to know at that point.

As the months go by in this phase of your relationship, your maturity level also increases. You start to develop deeper feelings, and your love grows into trust. You begin to start talking about more serious matters that will involve both of you and affect your lives together. You start to discuss more serious aspects of your relationship, whether it be something as simple as a bill that is hindering you or a promise you made to one of your friends or family that may interfere with something your mate has planned.

The dwindling honeymoon effects may leave you feeling less excited to hear from each other, and you may experience some slow and uneventful evenings and weekends. But that doesn't mean the relationship is over—it means you have to take time to show creativity and keep the flame lit. Think about what the other person enjoys doing, and schedule some fun-filled evenings and weekends—or just schedule a time for you to have a conversation and keep the lines of communication open. Remember, say and do it all in love, and you will develop a love that will deepen and keep you focused on each other throughout the course of your relationship.

VALECIA: Thinking back to our honeymoon phase, I remember the countless times we took long walks on the pier of Lake Michigan. We went everywhere together. Long drives up north, just looking at the countryside road and God's beautiful landscaping of the trees, flowers, fields, and blue skies and sunsets. We would go out for ice-cream cones or listen to soft music as we ate dinner by candlelight. I would watch fishing shows and the Packers football games, and I often went on fishing daytrips—all because we loved being with each other all the time. I was shocked that for years my husband would go with me to the hair salon and wait until I was done, without complaining. I know that was love, because at times we would be at the salon for three or four hours straight. We didn't have cell phones then, but we did have a 110 camera, and we made sure to take lots of pictures no matter what we were doing.

Genesis 2:23-24 (AMP) says:

> Then Adam said, "This is now bone of my bones, And flesh of my flesh; She shall be called Woman, Because she was taken out of Man." For this reason a man shall leave his father and his mother, and shall be joined to his wife; and they shall become one flesh.

Positive memories to reflect on during trying times
Use the space below to write out some memories you treasure.

BUILDING YOUR FOUNDATION

To build a strong foundation for your marriage, you must base it on some essential building blocks. According to *Becoming Minimalist* (www.becomingminimalist.com), these are love and commitment, sexual faithfulness, trust, honesty, communication, selflessness, quality time, humility, patience, and forgiveness. Let's go over a few of these key elements to give you an idea of what they can mean.

Love and commitment go hand in hand. When you love someone, naturally you want to commit to that person, and commitment contributes to a stable foundation. Sexual faithfulness grows from your love and commitment. Being sexually faithful with your mate means you are not being sexual with anyone other than your mate. Trust and honesty are necessary for a strong foundation because without trust there will be doubt. Honesty ties in with trust: if you are not honest with each other, your foundation will be shaky and lessen your trust.

After we were married, we became a blended family instantly. There were a lot of good times and some not so good times. Some of the children were only with us on weekends, which didn't give us much time to establish that family connection and trust. They would come Friday evenings and leave Sunday right after church. When they were not there, our home seemed incomplete, and at times only one or two would come. The stability was missing, and our foundation did not feel secure. We did not understand at the time what was going on, but as the children got older and started to voice their feelings, we found out that their mother was speaking ill of us, which caused a lot of division and unnecessary hurt. Despite all the negative lies she would tell the children, we always instilled values of love, honor, and respect for their mother in them. Although we did all we could to repair what was broken, the damage had already been done. There are still scars and uncertainty even though all our children are adults now. We love them all no matter what they believe from the lies they were told. That is why honesty is such an important part of your foundation.

Communication is essential because without it, you cannot build further. There are several aspects to what you say, and communication includes both what you say and how you listen. Ask yourself whether the way you communicate with your mate is effective. Do you listen without being defensive? Do you expect your mate to know what you feel or think without telling them? Do you talk over each other without letting the other person finish speaking? Be honest about your feelings and thoughts—you can't expect the other person to be able to read your mind. When expressing yourself, use more "I" statements and fewer "you" statements. For example, instead of saying "When you told me how you felt about the bills being paid and me overspending, you made me feel bad," try "When we were discussing bills and my overspending was the topic, I felt like my strategy and methods weren't acceptable, and that bothered me." Saying it the first way could come off as finger pointing, so be sure to consider your mate even when you feel uneasy about the circumstance.

Being compatible doesn't mean you will think and feel the same way about everything; however, selflessness is a quality you and your mate should possess, which will bring out a sense of empathy and compassion when most necessary. These traits are great to have for your own sake, but they are also valuable to your mate, who will reap the benefit of expressing them. You each have your own personality and a certain way you did things before you met, so always respect and embrace your differences. Sometimes minor accommodations will make everything all right. Never tear down your mate in private or in public, in the presence of family and friends, and especially not with your children there. Put yourself in your mate's shoes when there are situations you do not understand. Be compassionate toward each other, and express empathy when there are times of heartache and pain, such as the loss of their family member or a friend.

Be intentional about spending quality time together, but also be spontaneous and have a sense of humor. Spontaneity adds spice to your marriage, and a sense of humor brings laughter and fun. There must be a balance in all that you do. Take turns doing what the other likes—that's where selflessness and quality time meet. Quality family time, quality couple time, and quality time with yourself, which is known as self-care—you need these to be able to rest, relax, and release! If you don't love and care for yourselves as individuals, how will you be able to love and care for your family?

Honor your commitment as you vowed to do on your wedding day. Trust and continue to be trustworthy. Convey humility and accept that you need to make a change without complaining, extend patience as you would want it extended to you, and always give forgiveness—because if you don't forgive, how will you forget? If you don't, it will prevent you from moving forward. If there is any question about anything you are uncertain about, you should be honest and forthcoming about it in a calm, respectful and loving tone. You can express yourself without overstepping boundaries. Keep in mind that things are sweeter if you use sugar, not vinegar, so be sweet to your spouse or mate.

Are you and your spouse serving God? Are both of you allowing God to be in control of your lives? Are you following the path that God has laid before you? As husband and wife, you are a family. God's plan is for your family to know him completely and become part of his family. For this to happen, you must be of one accord and serve God as a whole unit. There cannot be one spouse serving God and the other straddling the fence. If this occurs, you are unequally yoked and will not receive your full blessing. You are in the same family as far as being husband and wife, but you will not be part of God's family wholeheartedly. For that to happen, you must be for God, not against God—nor can you be lukewarm, meaning stuck in the middle, because with God there is no middle.

Think about what your life would be like with or without God. Can you imagine not having his guidance after depending on him for direction? Can you imagine how much better you will be for having God's guidance than when you didn't have it before? Wherever you are in your state of mind, picture that, and ask yourself how you will or will not be affected by the change. Think about your reaction to the thought of it and how your life would be impacted. If you no longer had Christ and your life would not change, then you never had Christ as you thought you did. Christ's guidance, as with everything from Christ, is 100 percent, and everything we do without him is less than that.

VALECIA: I don't know about you, but we want 100 percent! When we got married, I was serving God and Walter was not. I could not understand how or why we struggled so much in our marriage, but as I continued to seek God more and more, it was revealed to me that my husband was the priest of our home, and we could not receive the full potential of our blessings because the priest of our home was not holy. After trusting God, praying for my husband, and continuing to stand in the gap for him, God turned my husband's life around. He took away the cigarettes my husband smoked since he was eighteen years old, and he took away the alcohol he had been consuming since that time also. I know it was because of my prayers and his desire to live for God. Through it all, God saw fit to bless us with his unmerited favor, and we are so thankful.

It is important to keep the lines of communication open. There are many different forms of communication, including talking, body language, texting, and actions, such as cooking your mate's favorite meal as an apology. You decide which ones work best for you. Let the circumstance determine what form of communication you use and the time to use it. When you are having a discussion, be sure to pay close attention to your mate and listen carefully to what is being said, so you have clarity. Listen twice as much as you speak. Make certain that you are speaking for yourself and not for your mate. Be mindful not to interrupt while the other is speaking. You will get your turn to speak, and you want your mate to extend the same manner of respect to you.

If you need to write down key points you want to address, that is fine. If you take notes as your mate is speaking, remember to look up now and then as you write, so you continue to acknowledge what your mate is saying. You don't want them to think you are not paying attention or ignoring what is being said.

Try to have meaningful conversations in person or over the telephone. If possible, please do not have these conversations by texting. The lines of communication may become blurred, as texting can be taken out of context at times, which can cause a whole other set of issues.

These are some key elements in building your foundation. If you find some things work, that is great, and if some things do not work, that is fine as well. Just remember to use what does work and continue to build from there. We are strong believers and hold true to the words "a family that prays together stays together!" It may sound like a cliché, but it has helped strengthen our marriage and has kept our foundation stable.

The scripture 1 Corinthians 3:11–17 (NIV) says:

> For no one can lay any foundation other than the one already laid, which is Jesus Christ. If anyone builds on this foundation using gold, silver, costly stones, wood, hay or straw, their work will be shown for what it is, because the Day will bring it to light. It will be revealed with fire, and the fire will test the quality of each person's work. If what has been built survives, the builder will receive a reward. If it is burned up, the builder will suffer loss but yet will be saved-even though only as one escaping through the flames. Don't you know that you yourselves are God's temple and that God's Spirit dwells in your midst? If anyone destroys God's temple, God will destroy that person; for God's temple is sacred, and you together are that temple.

Use this list of key elements for your foundation to see what you might need to work on, and then plan how to do it.

Foundations of your relationship
Love/commitment
Sexual faithfulness
Trust
Honest
Communication
Selflessness
Quality time
Humility
Patience
Forgiveness

CHAPTER 6

BUDGET OR BUST

It is a fact that marriages have faced turmoil and conflict due to poorly managed finances. Some have even been destroyed because of that. Make sure you are on the same page when it comes to your finances. You aren't alone, so consider your spouse when making financial decisions. There are a lot of factors that go into play where finances are concerned. There have been several elements that we considered while discussing our finances, so below are some examples.

Budgeting

Budgeting with your spouse is an extremely important decision that you make together. It helps you work toward your financial goals and generate more cash flow as you plan your financial future, as well as establish current financial stability.

Bill Payments

There are many bills to consider when you are alone but even more when you get married: food, rent or mortgage, transportation, and utilities, to name a few. Come up with a strategy for your bill payments. Create a list of your bills and organize them by date and with the amount due. You can handle your bill payment list on the computer if you like, using a spreadsheet or a table with columns and rows—or just write your list out on lined paper. Keep track to keep you from missing a payment and from suffering financially with those pesky late fees and penalties. Your bills are a high priority, so take charge and stay in control of them.

Allowances

Once bill payments are listed, you have a better idea of what you can save and what your allowances will look like. Think of saving as paying yourself. Save for that rainy day. As you build your savings, you can borrow from it when circumstances arise instead of borrowing from someone else, which we do not advise you to do. And you must pay yourself back, so you continue to reach your saving goals. This is good money management, so practice it and keep the momentum going. It is OK to have an allowance for each of you when you get paid if the bills are in order and you have contributed to your savings. Pocket change is nice—but not a necessity.

Bank Accounts

When you get married, something you must discuss is your bank account. In some marriages, the husband and wife keep their separate accounts and together contribute to bills, housing, food, and other expenses. Others may create a joint account, and deposit in the joint account, from which the bills are then paid. Some couples may dissolve their separate accounts and handle everything from one joint savings and checking account. No matter which way you decide to work out your bank account circumstances, there should be someone in charge of the finances for paying bills, so when matters need to be addressed someone is already delegated to handle the task.

VALECIA: In our household we decided that I would oversee our finances. I still write out our monthly budget in a composition book as well as on the computer. I just like to have a backup. I am old school, so it works for us. I can keep up with all our bills with this method without any issues. We discuss finances during our bimonthly family meeting to keep the lines of communication open and address any concerns.

Long- and Short-Term Goals

Once you have your bills under control and are secure in your budget, it would be a great time to write out your short- and long-term goals. This is where you will discuss such things as vacations, buying a home, or purchasing a vehicle. After you have discussed your plans for the near and farther future, get your creative genes together and make your vision board! Don't forget to put it up in a space where you will see it every day as a reminder for what you are aiming for. It is truly a great way to stay focused on reaching your goals one by one.

Credit

Before you get married, you should have a conversation about your credit and whether it is good or poor. Have you considered what your credit should look like to become a homeowner? Do either of you have outstanding debts, owe the IRS taxes, or have your paycheck garnished? These are serious eye-opening situations that can cause major issues in a marriage—his debt becomes hers, and her debt becomes his.

Great credit makes it easier for you to manage your finances, purchase a home, go on vacations, and purchase a new vehicle. When your credit is great, your interest rates are lower! If neither of you understand credit, it doesn't hurt to get credit counseling. If you have credit cards, you will want to keep your utilization rate at nothing higher than 30 percent monthly. Pay your credit card bills before you are charged interest fees if you can, but if you can't pay off the balance immediately, pay on or before the due date. We recommend that you pay more than your minimum due. If we don't pay off our cards, we pay half of the total balance or double our payments. With good credit, you have a good name, and with a good name, you can get whatever you want and need. So great credit is something worth placing on your vision board.

VALECIA: I can tell you now that I was clueless about all of this when I said "I do." At tax time, I was looking forward to a nice fat lump sum from my federal filing, and instead I received a letter that said "Intercepted." I was livid! I called the IRS and found out it was for my husband's child support order. I was shocked, because he was paying his child support. However, there were arrears, so they took all our refund. I had to file an amendment with an injured spouse form, and we were able to get half of our taxes back, but that took twelve weeks. Thank God that is over with now!

When you get in a position where your finances are stable and you are building your savings, do not get sidetracked or lose focus on continuing to strengthen your finances. We had a season of financial stability, and earning money was on the rise. We began to be careless with money, and it caused things to go wrong.

I want to share with you a scenario where we lost sight of our purpose with money for a little while. When we had a home improvement company and a daycare, we had money coming in fast, and when it came down to us discussing the finances, we started to bump heads. I think we were both on an ego trip or something. One day we went to the bank to make a large deposit. We had just completed a Harambee job and a city job, and I wanted to go shopping, so we took $5,000 in cash with us.

We were having a conversation about how I was concerned about us spending wisely and not going overboard and buying unnecessary items. Walter got irritated with me because I usually shop and buy what I want, and he barely says anything about it. We were going on and on about the $5,000, when he suddenly said, "I don't care about this money," and took the entire $5,000 and tossed it out the car window. With the car still in motion, our daughter jumped out and grabbed every $100 bill he tossed. I could not believe he did that, and after that shocking tactic *I* kept the money, so he wouldn't get any more of his bright ideas.

The point is that when you increase your finances and build your savings, don't take money for granted because it will not always be there for you to do as you need or want.

Luke 14:28–30 (ESV) says:

> For which of you, desiring to build a tower, does not first sit down and count the cost, whether he has enough to complete it? Otherwise, when he has laid a foundation and is not able to finish, all who see it begin to mock him, saying, "This man began to build and was not able to finish."

We have included a budget sheet to assist you with your planning, and an organizing list for long- and short-term goals.

The _____ Family Budget
(Name)

Monthly income	Expected	Actual	Difference
Income 1	$	$	$
Income 2	$	$	$
Total	$	$	$
Monthly expenses	**Budgeted**	**Actual**	**Difference**
HOME			
Mortgage/rent	$	$	$
Electric/gas	$	$	$
Water/sewage/trash	$	$	$
Cell phone/landline/cable/internet	$	$	$
Cleaning supplies	$	$	$
Toiletries	$	$	$
Other	$	$	$
Total	$	$	$
FOOD			
Groceries	$	$	$
School lunches	$	$	$
Work lunches	$	$	$

Other	$	$	$
Total	$	$	$
TRANSPORTATION			
Car payment	$	$	$
Car insurance	$	$	$
Gasoline	$	$	$
Repairs/maintenance	$	$	$
Public transportation	$	$	$
Other	$	$	$
Total	$	$	$
OTHER EXPENSES			
Health and wellness/medical/ prescriptions	$	$	$
Childcare	$	$	$
Child support	$	$	$
Clothing and shoes	$	$	$
Personal hygiene/grooming	$	$	$
Fitness/gym memberships	$	$	$
Entertainment/outings/Netflix etc.	$	$	$
Other	$	$	$
Total	$	$	$

Making lists can help you organize the goals you want to achieve. Setting a date, such as a month and a year, creates a target for making your goals a reality. For short-term goals, you might be as specific as the day, month, and year; for long-term goals, you might be able to project only the year of completion. Short-term examples would include travelling or paying off small debts; long-term examples might be family planning, or paying off large debts.

Short-term goals   Date to achieve

1. _____

2. _____

3. _____

4. _____

5. _____

6. _____

7. _____

8. _____

9. _____

10. _____

Long-term goals   ## Date to achieve

1. _____

2. _____

3. _____

4. _____

5. _____

6. _____

7. _____

8. _____

9. _____

10. _____

THE IN-AND-OUT PHASE

Think about how you feel when you meet someone new. In the beginning, you are infatuated with that person. You are all *in* and full of excitement. That is the comfortable or "in" phase. But through the course of your relationship, you will have tests and trials that can make you want to give up. This is the "out" phase—you are no longer in the space where you are all in. This is an extremely challenging phase to go through, and it can occur at any time, and sometimes multiple times, and in many different forms. Because of your infatuation, you may decide to stick it out until you resolve the matter at hand. That's why we call this the "in and out" phase of the relationship, and it can make you or break you. How you handle it, what you say, and what you do will determine whether the relationship survives. Throughout the course of a relationship, you will have different obstacles to face that can have you in and out, and you may go back and forth. In the end, you will either stay together and soldier through the situation, or bid farewell to each other, temporarily or for good!

During our in-and-out phase, we went through in and out so many ins and outs it would be impossible to tell about them all. This phase is about the battles with your hang-ups. What is it that you need to be delivered from? Whatever it is, you cannot do it on your own. You need the Lord to deliver you from your sins and from other hang-ups that may not be sins but are damaging to your relationship, such as hanging out with unsavory associates or friends of the opposite sex, smoking, drinking, or missing important events with your spouse. These are all examples that may put you on the "out," so consider your mate during this time and be more mindful. Discuss the circumstance and come to an understanding or compromise.

Think about everything you need to be delivered from and everything that has hindered you or kept you from moving forward. It might be drugs, alcohol, cigarettes, lust, emotional infidelity, lying, stealing—anything that keeps you from prospering in your marriage or your relationship with God. There might be negative sparks from your past that arise, such as an old abusive relationship, sexual assault from the past, or abandonment issues. These are serious issues that you need to let your spouse know about, because if they resurface and affect your memory or behavior, they can cause problems quickly if you don't resolve them together. If you tackle them together one by one, you can limit the length of time you are in this phase and eliminate it from resurfacing. So cut it off right away!

You want to be mindful not to go back to your hang-ups and the sins you asked God to deliver you from. When you let go, walk in your deliverance. When you are tempted to fall back into any of them, remember that if you choose to go back and pick up what God has delivered you from, you will bring more negative spirits along with the ones you let go of initially. If you ask God to deliver you from alcohol and you go back to drinking it again, that spirit of alcohol will bring seven more negative spirits, and they will enter in your body and stay there. Then you will have eight negative spirits to struggle with, along with whatever else you are already dealing with.

Have you had a discussion with your mate about conflict resolution when you are faced with circumstances that aren't so pleasant, and how you will overcome them together? Have you ever thought about what would happen if you were in a situation that you always said you would never put up with or accept from anyone? We ask these questions because when you get married sometimes these are topics that aren't discussed. When you are young and you see someone going through a situation, the first thing you say without thinking about it is, "I will never deal with anything like that!" or "There is no way I will let my husband or wife do that or say that to me!" You may have even said, "Why don't she or he just get a divorce?" It is so easy to say things like this when you are young and don't know any better, or when you are older and understand but aren't the main character in the story.

If you have not spoken about what you will do to resolve the more serious issues you may face, we suggest you seek counseling from your spiritual leader, your pastor, or someone your pastor may appoint. If you do not have a church home, you may want to connect with a church and speak with their pastor for direction.

During the in-and-out phase, there may be a problem that will have you contemplating leaving your marriage, but before you react from your emotions, please weigh your options. Don't make a decision based solely on those emotions, because you will regret it in the end. This is a very trying phase to be in, and you may find yourself in this phase more than once throughout your marriage. That's normal. It is all about what you can handle and overcome, so you both can resolve it, move past it, and continue to grow so your marriage can be successful.

VALECIA: When I was young and clueless, I would say things like, "When I get married my husband better not say this or do that, because I will not let him!" I also remember saying that I would not stay in a marriage if there were a lot of problems, but when you know God and how he feels about marriage, you change your way of thinking. God wants us to seek him in everything, and that includes when you are faced with trials and tribulations.

There have been a lot of in-and-out moments during our marriage, and although they were unpleasant, they helped us grow. It showed me how strong we are as individuals and as supportive spouses to each other even during the rough times. So let me tell you a little more about our in-and-out phase.

Alcohol was a major hang-up during this phase for us. When Walter would drink, he would stay out late or not come home at all. One Thanksgiving Eve, I was livid that Walter was not home. I was cooking for the holiday, and he was missing in action. After I had stood at the sink cleaning chitterlings for hours on end, he finally walked in the door with his Coogi sweater and his matching Coogi hat. When he came in the kitchen, I just continued to clean the chitterlings like he wasn't there, but I could smell the alcohol on his breath a mile away. He came and stood next to me, then put his hand in the water and splashed the water that the chitterlings were in right in my face. So I took a chitterling, and I threw it on him. He grabbed a handful of the chitterlings I had cleaned from the bowl and he threw them. They hit me in the face, so I took the bucket with the scum I had cleaned out of the chitterlings and dumped it on him—and the chitterling fight was on! Before I knew it, we were throwing chitterlings back and forth and they ended up all over the kitchen. It was the most disgusting food fight ever, and the kitchen reeked, so Walter cleaned and sanitized the entire kitchen and everything in it.

For those of you who don't know what chitterlings are, they are pig intestines. Needless to say, we haven't eaten a chitterling since our infamous Chitterling Fight.

This is just one circumstance of our in-and-out phase, before we finally started to get it right. It was a time when we were in our out phase, and not only was it ridiculous, it was embarrassing and flat-out wrong that we behaved this way. And we did it in front of our children! We had to apologize to them and let them know the way we acted was inappropriate and would never happen again.

Matthew 12:43–45 says:

> When the unclean spirit is gone out of a man, he walketh through dry places, seeking rest, and findeth none. Then he saith, I will return into my house from whence I came out; and when he is come, he findeth it empty, swept, and garnished. Then goeth he, and taketh with himself seven other spirits more wicked than himself, and they enter in and dwell there: and the last state of that man is worse than the first. Even so shall it be also unto this wicked generation.

Hang-ups that may cause "outs"	

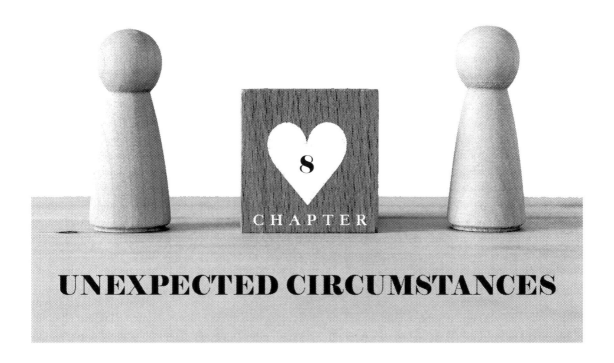

UNEXPECTED CIRCUMSTANCES

When you get married, there are some unexpected circumstances—situations that arise when you did not see them coming—that may change your entire life. Changes are not necessarily bad; however, changes can make your lifestyle different, so it is important to get to know your mate and talk about your lives and what that means for your future together.

Let's talk about one example to give you some insight into what we mean by unexpected circumstances: the blended family, when one spouse or both will be bringing a child or children into the marriage. When you get married, you are accepting your spouse and any children your spouse may have already. You cannot like the tree and not love the apples that fall off of it.

VALECIA: Our home that had consisted of one child soon became a home of four children after we were married, which meant major changes had to be made. My husband and I had a conversation after we were married, because circumstances in the life of his children's mother called for our immediate attention. Long story short, we ended up getting primary placement of his three children.

For us to maintain our home, there had to be organization and structure. I had a checklist of chores and all that needed to be done for each chore, and a chart to assign chores, so I knew who was responsible for each chore on which day. The children hated my detailed chore list, as you can imagine, but I loved it. It left no room for them to say "I forgot" or "I didn't know what to do"—my list explained what to do and *how* to do it.

We had family meetings twice a month, and of course family outings and movie nights at home. It was better having all the children there consistently instead of weekends and holidays only. Our blended family was an unexpected circumstance, but it worked for us.

If you are blessed with a blended family, make the most of it. Love all the children and treat them all fairly. Keep the lines of communication open, so all parents are aware; however, do not let the children's other parent disrupt your household. Your immediate family consists of those who live in your home and that is you, your spouse, and all your children.

When we had our family meetings, it was a time for everyone to speak and be heard. Everyone should have an outlet for being heard and feel able to voice their feelings and thoughts. Our biweekly meetings were aimed at providing the perfect atmosphere. Our rule was that you could say what you like, as long as you were respectful, talking not yelling, and listening until it was your turn to talk.

How you introduce your children to your spouse will weigh heavy if you aren't careful in how you do it. We never forced the children to call us Mom or Dad. They did it on their own, and they respected who we were even if they didn't call us Mom or Dad all the time. Whenever we addressed our children, we never said "stepchildren," "stepmom," or "stepdad." We addressed them as our children, and they addressed us as their parents, because that's how it was and still is with us.

What are some other unexpected circumstances? So many families struggle with health issues and injuries. Have you considered what would happen if your spouse got ill or seriously injured? Do you both have health insurance? How will you manage your lifestyle if this were to happen? This isn't anybody's favorite topic for discussion, but it is a topic that is necessary to discuss.

Life insurance is extremely important, and you should have it for yourself, your spouse, and your children. You do not want your loved ones to be left with the burden of struggling to pay bills and so on while mourning the loss of you. You should also have a living will, so if something were to happen and you aren't able to speak for yourself, your living will can explain everything you want and eliminate the stress of family trying to decide what they think is best for you. And get your pre-planning in order with the funeral home and cemetery, so everything will be set up and in place when that time comes. Again, this is not a pleasant conversation, but it is necessary.

Let's look at one more unexpected circumstance: caring for a loved one. Have you thought about what might happen if one of your parents, siblings, grandparents, grandchildren, or other relatives needs to be cared for? Would you feel comfortable with them being in a nursing home, foster home, or other care facility, or will you care for them in your home? How will this impact your marriage? You must be of one accord in deciding how you will care for your loved one—or whether you will do it at all. If you do, you and your spouse will have to decide how to care for the loved one and how you will alternate care. How will your home be set up to accommodate your loved one so they can be comfortable? These are questions you will have to answer together, so you can agree and know what to expect from each other.

We had been looking forward to being empty nesters when our youngest child was about to turn eighteen and was thinking about college or serving in the military. But before we could experience being empty nesters, our grandson Jewell was placed in our care by the Department of Children and Family Services. His birth was premature, and he had been in the neonatal intensive care unit for three and a half months. When released from the hospital, he still had chronic lung disease and was on oxygen all day and night, among other illnesses he faced through his growth and development. We have had him in our care since he was six months old, and as we write this book, he is six years old. We had to make a lot of changes and adjustments to accommodate our little Prince Jewell, and we are thankful to God for blessing us with the ability to make the necessary changes for him. He is such a fighter, and he loves Jesus Christ just as we do.

There are other unexpected circumstances that you may experience, and some can be serious, like the loss of a job or a pandemic, or a traffic jam, which may not be serious but can be annoying. Whether serious or not so serious, unexpected circumstances are the things you have no control over, and many of them will require you and your mate to have a heart-to-heart conversation so you can put your heads together and make some decisions.

Proverbs 3:5–7 (KJV) says:

> Trust in the Lord with all thine heart; and lean not unto thine own understanding. In all thy ways acknowledge him, and he shall direct thy paths. Be not wise in thine own eyes: fear the Lord and depart from evil.

List some unexpected circumstances you have encountered and how you faced those challenges together.

Unexpected Circumstances	Resolution

INTIMATE MOMENTS

For many people, intimacy means sex; however, intimacy can be as simple as sweet little things your spouse does or says to see you smile. It can be gentle touches, like a back rub, playing footsie, or running your fingers through their hair. Holding your spouse closely at night as they sleep. Just being together laughing and talking. These are all forms of intimacy, but it does not stop with the physical or even the emotional. Intimacy is a sense of being close and passionately connected and supported. It means being able to share an entire range of ideas, thoughts, feelings, and experiences together.

Intimacy encourages a stronger connection and builds a stronger friendship. Your spouse or mate should be your best friend. There should be nothing you cannot share with each other. Intimacy is an important act you share in a relationship.

There is nothing wrong with sexual intimacy, either! It is especially important to have a healthy sexual appetite in marriage. Being romantic and displaying intimate moments throughout your lives together will keep your marriage strong and full of excitement. Be mindful of each other and keep the lines of communication open, so that during times that test your relationship you are both aware of what one another needs and want.

Men mainly respond in the physical, and women mostly in the emotional. It's natural. It's the way each gender is made up. We all need love and want to be understood, so it's important for a husband to understand his wife, and for a wife to understand her husband. Be patient and compassionate with your spouse and their wants and needs, whether physical or emotional. Your needs won't be the same, but they should not go unattended or unsatisfied.

"Pillow talk" is the relaxed physical conversation that usually occurs after sex, with cuddling, rubbing, and kissing. You need to make a commitment in your marriage to have pillow talk! It will boost your intimacy and spice up your romance. It helps to build your communication skills and adds to your quality time together.

There are a lot of things that can light the fire of your intimacy, and the more you know about each other, the better. Knowing what your spouse enjoys eating, where they enjoy going, and what type of movies they like to watch are pieces of information that will gain you points when it comes to planning a surprise dinner or outing. Create a list of what you like to eat, where you like to go, and what simple pleasures make you smile and swap your list with one another.

The charts below are to assist you with sharing your likes with each other so your mate can be more fully aware of what you want, need, and desire. There's one chart for her and one for him. Make it clear what your favorite outings are, or your favorite restaurants for dining in or takeout. When listing your simple pleasures, keep in mind that the little things count—your favorite snacks or your preferred essential oil. These lists will help you both when you want to surprise the other with a "just because" gift, plan something special for a birthday, or celebrate other occasions, so take your time and enjoy this assignment.

Her favorite outings	Favorite restaurants (dine-in or takeout)	Simple pleasures

His favorite outings	Favorite restaurants (dine-in or takeout)	Simple pleasures

Take this time also to create a calendar to arrange your date nights and family nights. You may even want to list your self-care dates on the calendar, so you don't forget to take care of yourself. If you take care of *you*, you can take better care of your spouse and your children! We can't stress that enough. Self-care is important. You can use the following date-night calendar to organize your areas of caring.

Date Night Calendar

Date	Time	Outing

At the same time, spontaneity keeps your relationship alive. In your lives together, you will develop traditions, and some things will become routine, but because you are both constantly changing as you grow older together, it's essential to grow new interests together, so you don't grow apart or feel like you don't know each other anymore. Spontaneity will keep things interesting and that flame burning strong. Either of you can take the lead by being spontaneous at any given moment and as often as you like.

One example is surprise "just because" gifts—nothing expensive, and you can even make one, whether or not you're creative. It's the thought behind the gift! Write your spouse a poem or love note, and put it in their lunch or in a spot they will see it. Arrange for the children to be settled with a sitter or have something to occupy them while you plan a "staycation" in your bedroom or other private space in your home. Play some music, make a soft comfy pallet on the floor, have a picnic with or without a picnic basket, and enjoy each other all night. Or surprise your spouse with a date night and take the weight off by doing the dishes, mopping the floor, or cooking dinner.

Now take some time and think about what your spouse might like that you can do on the spur of the moment. Being spontaneous feels like the excitement of that beautiful finale at the end of a fireworks show—everyone I know loves the fireworks finale—but it's good to have some tricks up your sleeve in advance. We've offered several examples of how to create intimate moments for you in this lesson, but you have to find your niche and know what works for you.

First Corinthians 13:13 (NLT) says, "Three things will last forever—faith, hope, and love—and the greatest of these is love." So one way we like to share love is by giving each other love coupons. Love coupons are a sure way to ignite your marriage and boost your romance. A love coupon shows your spouse that you are thinking about them, want quality time with them, and absolutely love them. These tokens of love can help you make time for lovemaking and build on the success of your marriage, especially if you have children. You know your spouse best, so be creative and spontaneous—the love coupons we offer below can be personalized for you and your spouse. So here are some love coupons to get you started, and enjoy filling in the blanks!

Love Coupon

You are entitled to Breakfast in Bed!

Name: _____

Love Coupon

You are entitled to a ½ hour Back rub!

Name: _____

Love Coupon

You are entitled to _____

Name: _____

THE MARRIAGE PLAN

Now that we've covered various aspects of marriage, we encourage you to pull them all together in support of a marriage plan for your personal guide. This document will help you both see your marriage more clearly so you can ensure your priorities are the same as you both grow.

According to Wikipedia, "a business plan is a formal written document containing the goals of a business, the methods for attaining those goals, and the time-frame for the achievement of the goals. It also describes the nature of the business, background information on the organization, the organization's financial projections, and the strategies it intends to implement to achieve the stated targets. In its entirety, this document serves as a road-map (a plan) that provides direction to the business." A written business plan—a guide to how the business will operate from the beginning on to the future—is the foundation for successful businesses.

We believe that a marriage plan will help you in that same manner. If you fail to prepare, you are preparing to fail. So write out your marriage plan, sign it, and follow it to completion. Use the marriage plan to keep you accountable as you work to reach your relationship goals.

To get started on your marriage plan, set aside a nice amount of time for the both of you in a secluded place without any distractions. Maybe consider a weekend getaway or a staycation, without children, television, cell phone, social media or anyone or anything that will keep you from focusing on your marriage plan. Stay on task and be diligent about completing your marriage plan. It is the guide to your successful marriage/relationship. Next, spend some time praying and discussing the categories of your life and use extra paper if you need to.

If you do as Habakkuk 2:2 (KJV) says, "And the Lord answered me, and said, 'Write the vision, and make it plain upon tables, that he may run that readeth it,'" you will see progress and ultimately success. It is essential to write down your thought-out vision so you have full and constant access to it.

We offer an online course that will lead you through all the steps to completing your marriage plan, along with free coaching sessions and other amenities to add spice to your relationship. The Marriage Plan online course is for married couples, those who are engaged, or singles who aspire to be married. It is available on our website, abovetheheart.net, so please do not slack on this amazing tool for the success of your marriage. It will help you take your marriage or relationship to the next level.

Marriage is a wonderful entity, but marriage is work! You will get out what you put in, so be persistent. This is a vow you took standing before God, and he honors your marriage.

We've come to the end of the final chapter, so we want to leave you with our ten basic principles of marriage and marriage coaching. We suggest you read them daily to get them in your heart and mind so you can apply them to your life. We love you with the love of God and pray for an abundance of blessings and prosperity in your marriage or relationship together in Jesus name, amen!

Ten Principles for Marriage and Marriage Coaching

1. Keep putting Jesus first; keep loving Jesus most.
2. Be empowered, changed, and comforted by the Trinity. Be filled by the Spirit, empowered by the Son, and comforted by the Father.
3. Remember who your enemy is: Satan!
4. Take personal responsibility.
5. Take the log out of your own eye (Matthew 7:5), confess, and repent.
6. Forgive each other, reaffirm your love, and comfort each other.
7. Speak life-words, not death-words, to your spouse.
8. Put the interests of your spouse first in the power of Christ Jesus.
9. The husband should shepherd the wife with Christ's sacrificial, other-centered Love.
10. The wife should respectfully love the husband just as the church loves Christ Jesus.

Acknowledgments

♥ ♥ ♥ ♥ ♥ ♥

We acknowledge God for choosing us to be his vessel and using us to help those who want to take their marriage or relationship to the next level. As God leads, we will continue to follow the path that he has paved for us by way of Jesus Christ.

We would also like to acknowledge everyone who encouraged us or prayed for us on our marriage ministry journey. It may have been a phone call, a text message, or a visit from you, but in any case we are grateful for you and your loving kindness.

There have been so many people who have called on us for advice and help in their marriage, and we appreciate you entrusting us with such delicate and confidential information. Your belief in our strategies has proven that they work—if *you* are willing to work it. For all of you who continue to stand, we commend you for choosing to fight for your marriage.

Scriptures Cited

♥ ♥ ♥ ♥ ♥ ♥

These are the scriptures we have used as guidance in this book. We have found the Bible Gateway (www.biblegateway.com) to be a handy and invaluable way to compare versions of the Bible. As you study your Bible for its relationship wisdom, you may want to add to this list by making a note of scriptures that are meaningful to you. Come back to this list when you feel in need of God's words for you.

We use various versions of the Bible because in our studies we have found many ways to interpret the same scripture. The language in some versions is more simplified and gives us a better understanding. We encourage you to find the version that gives you clarity in your reading.

Ecclesiastes 4:9–12 (New Living Translation)
Ephesians 5:22–26 (New International Version)
Proverbs 18:22 (Amplified Bible)
Colossians 3:12–14 (New American Standard Bible)
Joshua 24:15 (Amplified Bible)
Genesis 2:23–24 (Amplified Bible)
1 Corinthians 3:11–17 (New International Version)
Luke 14:28–30 (English Standard Version)
Matthew 12:43–45 (King James Version)
Proverbs 3:5–7 (King James Version)
1 Corinthians 13:13 (New Living Translation)
1 Peter 3:1–2 (Amplified Bible)
Jeremiah 29:11 (New Living Translation)
Habakkuk 2:2 (King James Version)

About the Authors

♥ ♥ ♥ ♥ ♥ ♥

VALECIA CARTER was born in Milwaukee, Wisconsin, and was raised there in a two-parent household with her three siblings. From the age of eighteen, it was her dream to be happily married to the love of her life. She fulfilled her dream of being married August 3, 1996, but her happily-ever-after was in doubt for the first fifteen years of her marriage. There were many difficult situations she faced throughout those years. Her faith seemed to be tested at every turn. She found some solace in journaling year after year. After many struggles, she wanted to give up, so after having her husband served with divorce papers, she asked God to help her through the process. She was not prepared to be a divorcée with children, but she was fed up with trying to make what seemed like a failed marriage work. But once she stopped trying to fix her marriage herself, she asked God what she should do, and God told her to stand still and pray for her husband and her circumstances.

Valecia's first book, *My Heart, My Love, My Life, My Lord: Living Life Past the Pain* was written to help women and men who struggle in relationships know they can overcome their circumstances. Her book won the 2019 Christian Indie Award in the Nonfiction Christian Living category, and she was a recipient of the Off the Shelf Book Club Author's Award that same year.

WALTER CARTER was born in Attala, Mississippi, and was raised in Milwaukee by his mother with his four siblings until he was 16, when he moved out on his own. He was a young man determined to make something of himself and eventually to find his wife and be married. When he met Valecia Harris, he intuitively knew she was marriage material and made her his wife. He had some hang-ups that he was not aware of until they started weighing on his marriage. Not knowing how to handle unforeseen challenges soon put a strain on the marriage in the beginning and for fifteen years thereafter. Being served with divorce papers was a wake-up call: he knew that he did not want to lose his family, especially for something he could change.

WALTER AND VALECIA CARTER overcame their obstacles and many more by the power of God. They are grateful for the blessing God granted them by restoring their marriage. Together they have seven children and twenty grandchildren. They continue to express their love and devotion to each other daily. They are certified marriage coaches, podcasters, and motivational speakers. They launched their business Above the Heart LLC on February 15, 2019. Their vision is to help bond families through marriage and to restore, enrich, and encourage teens, singles, and couples by improving the present and enhancing their future. The mission of Above the Heart is to provide quality marriage and relationship education, to teach healthy relationship skills, and to help people embrace their uniqueness through strategic methods of reaching goals, becoming accountable, and enjoying a better and more fulfilling lifestyle. The City of Milwaukee Mayor issued a proclamation that as of June 8, 2019, every June 8 will be Above the Heart LLC Day.

For information about public-speaking bookings, book purchases, and The Marriage Plan online course, please go to the Above the Heart LLC website at abovetheheart.net or email abovetheheart0803@gmail.com.

Printed in the United States
by Baker & Taylor Publisher Services